PARENTING TEENS IN
A DIGITAL WORLD

RACHEL SIMMONDS

PARENTING TEENS IN A DIGITAL WORLD

publisher logo
The Oak Tree Press

CONTENTS

Acknowledgments
5

Foreword by Rebecca Jordan
7

Introduction
10

Part 1:

1 — Let Them Question Without Your Judgment
16

2 — Chores, Chores, Chores!
20

3 — Don't Hide Behind Devices
24

4 — Teach Compassion and Empathy
28

5 — If You Mess Up, Apologize!
32

CONTENTS

6 — Gratitude Is a Great Attitude
35

7 — Growth Mindset > Fixed Mindset
38

Part 2:

8 — Be Involved—but Not TOO Involved!
44

9 — If They Are Struggling—HELP!
48

10 — Partner with Teachers
51

11 — School Is a Priority and a Privilege
54

12 — Integrity Is a Must
59

Part 3:

13 — What Age Should I Give My Child a Phone?
64

14 — No Electronics in the Bedroom
68

15 — Whose Property Is It?
72

16 — Digital Addiction Is on the Rise
76

CONTENTS

17 — Social Media Overview
80

18 — The Challenges of Social Media
89

19 — Cyberbullying
93

20 — Restrictions
97

21 — How Teens Hide What They're Doing
100

22 — The Zoom World
104

23 — My Interview with Dr. Elizabeth Milovidov
108

24 — Final Thoughts
116

Bibliography
119

Parenting Teens in a
Digital World
by Rachel Simmonds

The Oak Tree Press
theoaktreepress.com

Library of Congress Cataloging-in-Publication Data
Names: Simmonds, Rachel, author.
Title: Parenting Teens in a Digital World – United States /
Rachel Simmonds
Identifiers:
LCCN: 2020918482
Paperback ISBN: 978-1-7351354-1-0
e-book ISBN: 978-1-7351354-0-3
Subjects: LCSH: Parenting | Technology
1st edition, November 2020
Printed in the United States of America
Cover by Jessie Rae Jordan

The Oak Tree Press
theoaktreepress.com

Thank you to my beautiful children Rebecca, Jessie, and Jack for always believing in me and pushing me to pursue my dreams. Thank you to Eric for supporting me and taking over some of the household duties while I worked on this book.

I also want to dedicate this to my mom, dad, sisters, and brother who love me unconditionally and have always believed in me. I'm grateful for all of you.

"Do the best you can until you know better. Then when you know better, do better."
—Maya Angelou

Acknowledgments

Ten years ago, I said I wanted to write a book. Then life got in the way with distractions, a cross-country move, and a new job, leaving that "becoming an author" idea a slowly burning ember inside of me that never saw the light of day.

My oldest daughter, Rebecca, who happens to be a brilliant writer, kept persistently nudging me over the years.

"Mom, what about that book you want to write?"

"So, Mom, have you thought about starting that book?"

"Hey, Mom, now with this pandemic, you have some time to write a book—don't you think?"

To be honest, I had been thinking about a topic for my book. So, in response to Rebecca's last question, I sat my family down and told them my idea. I felt I had enough experience and wisdom to give my thoughts on building solid relationships within a family in a modern world. They loved the concept.

The next day, as I was scrolling through Facebook, I came across my friend Gahmya Drummond-Bey's ad for a virtual writing retreat. I love when synchronicity is at play, and I never question it. I immediately signed up, and it was one of the best "5-second rule" moments of my life. If you don't know what the 5-second rule is, please read the book by Mel Robbins, but to simplify, it's counting down from 5 seconds to follow your instinct and make a quick decision. This type of decision-making is typically the best kind—where we push past a fear and make a giant step in our professional or emotional development.

So, thank you to Rebecca for staying on me throughout the years and Jessie, Eric, and Jack for being enthusiastic about my plan and supporting me from day one.

I would also like to thank my family and friends for being the first to jump at the chance to buy my book before it was even finished. They are: Kara Allaire, Leo Arteche, Tabitha Blue, Leah Bomar, Susan Bresth, Karen Bryant, Kerri Busch, Christine Clevenger, Jennifer Cool, Anna DaSilva, Eddie De La Vega, Matthew Goldberg, Nico Guggino, Stacie Hamilton, George and Tania Harkins, Sarah Harris, Kim Highsmith, Sam Hohn, Latrese Jackson, Robin Johnson, Heather Kathleen, Brittany Lane, Courtney Larsen, Veronika Levine, Michael Nesmith, Bridget Olson, Tonya Parker, Joshua Perez, Keri Lyn Shosted, Marisa Simmonds, Michael and Jessie Snyder, Christy Valdes, and Alana Wilson. Thank you, friends.

I want to extend a special thank you to Dr. Elizabeth Milovidov, a leading expert in eSafety, who was kind enough to talk to me and gracious enough to reassure me in my endeavors. I devoted an entire chapter to my interview with her.

I'd also like to thank Natalie Silver who edited my book, and Rebecca for reading it and assisting with content.

Last but not least, I could not have completed this book without the help of my mentor and dear friend Gahmya Drummond-Bey and our virtual writing group that met 3 days per week during the Covid-19 pandemic. We gathered from all over the world, via Zoom, carving out our books, bouncing ideas off one other, and supporting each another when fears would arise.

This book is a champion for all of you exhausted parents trying to hold it all together, who just want a solid relationship with your teens. *I see you; I hear you; I am one of you.*

Foreword by Rebecca Jordan

As the author of this book's firstborn and favorite child (I am absolutely kidding), I can say with confidence that my mother's words speak from true experience.

Growing up, I had a great childhood. It was filled with dolls, reading lots of books, trips to the beach, and sleepovers with cousins and friends. I was also an active participant in drama club throughout most of my grade school years. My world was exciting. Fun. And virtually...technology free.

Save for the occasional Tamagotchi birthday presents I would receive.

Of course, I will never forget the days when the Sidekick cell phone was all the rage. I begged and begged my mom to buy me one. My sister joined in on this and between the two of us, she would not hear the end of it.

"Why NAWT?! Mawwwwwm. Everyone has one."

"Good for them," she would tell us. And much to our disappointment, she would leave it at that.

Every.

Single.

Time.

It wasn't until I was 11 years old (and had the privilege of attending a private school) that I'd been handed my first ever big girl piece of technology.

A laptop computer.

My mom, as you'll read in this book, was *immediately* on top of this. She made sure that every single night before I went to bed, I turned in that laptop and any other technology I had laying around. Which wasn't really much, if anything. I do believe she let the Tamagotchis slide.

Then, when I finally turned 13, my mom did the thing she ALWAYS said she was going to do and gave me my first ever cellphone. SCORE!!! The phone was a sleek LG Shine that slid up and down. It only had a number keypad and terrible, if any, access to the internet...

I was so happy.

As I got older, the phones advanced. I would upgrade at the local AT&T store, and with every new phone I brought home, my mom would upgrade her parental skills as well.

By age 16, I discovered the wonderful worlds of Instagram and Facebook. As soon as I made an account, my mom made an account and followed me right away. Then I found Twitter; my mom created an account and followed me there too. Was it always preferred? Probably not. BUT did it prevent me from posting impulsive things that didn't need to be online, because I knew my mom was *watching* me? Most definitely.

In my senior year of high school, the technology rules I followed had finally paid off. My mom let me have a TV in my room, which was a huge deal, and let me use my laptop and phone as I wished.

That same year, I got accepted into my dream school: the Dodge College of Film and Media Arts Screenwriting program at Chapman University all the way across the country in Orange, California. And it honestly wasn't until after I finished reading this book, that I now understand achieving this incredible feat was very much attributed to my mother's strict technology rules.

Had she not confiscated my laptop every single night before bed, had she not stuck to her word and waited until I turned 13 to give me a phone, and had she not followed me on every social media platform I made an account on...I could have become so distracted and unable to keep my mind on track, that I could have not been able to move out of Florida to pursue my dreams!

And now, at the current age of 25 (living in my dream state of Southern California) I also realize that abiding by my mother's strict technology rules, has instilled a high level of responsibility when navigating the digital world within me. Virtual etiquette and maturity is a real thing. And it can get you very far in life (i.e. networking with people across the globe, promoting your own business, following accounts that motivate you, etc.)...or it can stunt your professional and personal growth.

So thank you, Mom, for putting up with me. With all your children. For putting your foot down and keeping it there. No matter how much we whined and complained about Sidekicks and computers and TVs. When you stuck to your word, good things came of it. This mama-warrior-spirit is what strongly inspires me to do the same when I raise my own children someday.

Seriously, Mom. Thank you for everything.

Parents reading this book, congrats you've found a winner. Clearly, there's more to the digital world today than there was when I was growing up, but my mother's updated guidelines with extremely detailed solutions for the world we live in today are so helpful— I didn't even know half of what she talks about existed until I read this!

And to give an extra nudge, my little brother just turned 13. So yeah, my mom really does know what she's talking about. She's as up to date as they come!

As for my sister and I, now both young adults...we turned out pretty good I'd say. ;)

Introduction

If you picked this book off the bookshelf, then you probably have a teen or soon-to-be teen and are wondering how to navigate this part of life. It's daunting. I know. I've been there.

So, why should you read this book? Why listen to me? I'm not a medical doctor or a therapist, and I don't claim to be an expert. BUT . . .

I'm a mother of three. I survived cycles of the teenage years with two moody, artsy daughters who are now thriving, successful adults and am currently beginning the teen years with my super smart, witty son.

Now you're probably thinking, so what? There are millions of mothers out there. Why should I listen to you?

Well, this is the thing.

I've taught middle school and high school students for *more than 20 years*. That alone should give me some sort of credibility (and should have earned me millions, but that's another argument for another day). I have seen and heard it all when it comes to teens and their parents, and I can, without a doubt, tell you what works and what doesn't.

I have been in the trenches. I have taught thousands of teenagers and have had hundreds of parent conferences.

I can always tell which students are given structure and routine at home and which are not. I can tell who has a good line of communication with their parent(s), and I can also identify who is given technology limitations and who is not.

I am sure many of my teacher friends would agree because it inevitably shows up in the classroom. The students with limits and boundaries most likely have good grades, are organized, and have incentive to do well.

Those who don't—well, let me just say that the frazzled home life typically shows up as a frazzled teen who is half asleep and doesn't know it's a test day. They can't find anything, are incredibly forgetful, and are the ones who repeatedly have missing assignments.

Now, I know there are other reasons why this may be, such as a learning disability or medical condition, but I'm speaking outside of that.

I see a pattern in why some teens are successful and why others are not. I don't just mean in academics—I mean at life. School is not for everyone, but it builds the foundation for skills that you work on throughout your life: grit, resilience, initiative, confidence, responsibility, and organization.

But it all starts at home.

Boundaries become difficult to establish if you've already had a laissez-faire attitude at home. However, the adage applies: better late than never!

I want to preface this book by explaining that I am NOT anti-technology. In fact, I love it. I've been learning and using technology since its inception, and I incorporate it into my classroom and enjoy it at home.

There are so many positive aspects to technology—communication, collaboration, education, and advances in medicine and science.

On the contrary, I want technology to be a positive experience for everyone, but it's necessary for parents to be informed about the issues surrounding good digital citizenship.

Let me first say that when I set out to write this book, my intention was to focus solely on digital parenting and technology.

However, as I began to shape out the content, I realized that I needed to approach this topic in several layers and from different perspectives.

For instance, the first layer to this "cake" is about establishing good communication with your children. In this section, I am speaking to you from my "mom" point of view. This first level is critical before we can even move to layer two, which is education.

In the second section, I am speaking from my "teacher" hat and giving you some insight about how to establish a good partnership with your child's teachers and set them up for success.

I finally cover electronics in the third and final section from a joint mom/teacher perspective, but I also do some research for you and provide you with resources to investigate further. I think half the battle is just knowing where to look for answers.

I know parents are busy, so I purposely wrote this as a brief handbook with bite-sized information to lead you in the right direction in the most concise and effective way possible.

Throughout this book, I give you simple action plans that you can do right away with an explanation of the lesson learned, so you understand the *purpose* of the action and what your teen is learning from your action.

Ideally, these initiatives should be fostered early on in their development, so when the teen years do arrive, it will be a seamless transition.

Please understand that there is no parent shaming here. We all have unique relationships with our children, and you know what works best for you and your child. My intention is to give you tools to help you make mindful choices about communicating with your child, fostering a love of education, and being an informed digital parent.

At the end of the book, you will find a list of resources that you can access that will assist you in delving more deeply into each topic if you choose to do so.

I wish you the best of luck as you embark on reading *Parenting Teens in a Digital World*!

PART 1:

Communication

LET THEM QUESTION WITHOUT YOUR JUDGMENT

This is *the most important* component in having a strong relationship with your teen. Without it, you're like a boat without a sail—just waiting for the next big wave to hit, with you and your teen flying overboard.

Good communication should build from early childhood, so you at least have a solid foundation. You'll notice as your child turns 9 and 10 (maybe even earlier) that conversations become more advanced and sometimes even comical.

"Mom, what's a [insert any embarrassing topic here]?"

Now, you can either freak out and scream that you never want to hear that word (or words) come out of their mouth ever again, or you can act like you are having a normal conversation.

What do you think will create a better sense of trust and openness with your child?

Why yell at them for something they never knew about? Why suppress their curiosity?

If children feel like they can't come to you for some honest answers, why do you think they'll come to you for anything?

I have had all kinds of questions thrown at me, and each time, I do my best to remain calm and answer them with as little or as much vocabulary a child of that age can handle.

Sometimes the questions can become quite uncomfortable, but your child is opening up to you as a source of trust. It's like confiding in you with the biggest secret imaginable.

Don't make them regret it.

There's nothing worse than a parent overreacting to a question, leaving a child to shudder in shame, embarrassed or afraid to ever ask another question.

Don't do this to them!

The same thing can be said about laughing.

There is nothing worse than being laughed at as a kid. I remember when I was young, and I tried to speak Spanish, and some of my older relatives would laugh at me thinking I was cute. I would make silly grammatical mistakes, but I felt bold enough to try.

Their laughter made me so embarrassed that I never tried to speak Spanish again—much to my parents' dismay, I refused. The thought of being laughed at was terrifying!

What may seem inconsequential or minor to you may seem like the world to your child. Their perspective is entirely different than yours as they are developing a sense of self and where they stand in the world.

It is imperative that you give them a comfortable space to grow and question without feeling judged. This is especially important when your child begins to navigate the digital space and may inadvertently stumble upon something inappropriate. Would you want your child to hide what they saw, or would you feel relieved that they feel comfortable enough to discuss it with you?

What if they are being approached by a cyberstalker or are being bullied by a classmate? If you've established a healthy line of communication, your child will be less apt to keep secrets from you. However, you will notice that by the time your child becomes a more independent adolescent, they will seek out their peers more in lieu of their parents for advice.

Keep in mind the high stakes of listening to your children and teens. The Office of Adolescent Health notes that "children who feel they are being heard will less likely engage in risky behaviors."

Although I love what technology can do for education and global communication, there are some negative consequences. There seem to be fewer face-to-face interactions within the family unit and less in-person socialization among friends.

Screens are sometimes taking the place of real one-on-one conversations.

Make sure your teen feels like it's fun to communicate with you. There's nothing better than laughter between parents and their teens. It feels free, open, and relaxed. I love to do silly things with my kids and throw around slang words, popular dances, or trends just to make their eyes roll.

PARENT ACTION PLAN: With your spouse, partner, or friend, practice having an uncomfortable conversation. Focus on your reactions—verbal and nonverbal. Watch those facial expressions!

CHILD'S LESSON LEARNED: I can count on my parents to be honest and truthful with me. I feel secure in my relationship with them.

CHORES, CHORES, CHORES!

When your teen feels that you understand them, or are at least trying to understand them, a whole new element of your relationship reveals itself. It's not about being the "cool" parent. It's about knowing how to have fun—with boundaries.

I think this is where the lines get kind of blurry for some parents. They believe that they can and should be best friends with their teens. *Nope*. They have plenty of friends. They need a parent. A parent who will set boundaries, give consequences, and be all up in their business, if necessary, to ensure their safety.

Parents, I know you want your children to have a better life than you did but remember that your job is *not* to make sure your kids have it easy.

Why don't a lot of kids have chores anymore? I always ask my students "Who has chores at home?" And every year, most of them don't. I don't get it. I believe chores should be mandatory for all children and teens. And it shouldn't always be for money.

Early in my teaching career, I noticed my students wanting to know what they got out of helping me with something, whether it was cleaning up the bookshelves, wiping down the whiteboards, or handing out papers—"Mrs. Simmonds, can I get extra credit or a homework pass?"

I would reply, "No, but you get the pleasure of knowing that you helped me."

They looked at me like I had three heads, but this is the problem. A lot of teens feel that doing something for others isn't worth it if they don't get anything tangible from it.

How can we raise a society of selfless, benevolent people if they only see what they can get materialistically from it?

This needs to start at home.

Chores don't have to be a miserable experience. I remember growing up and my mom cranking up some loud music in the house while we all helped clean. She either played loud salsa or Motown as we dusted and vacuumed the house, shaking our hips and trying out crazy dance steps while we laughed. Those are some memories that I cherish.

Children need to realize any mess they make is their responsibility. I can't tell you how many times I've had students leave their trash on their desks for me to pick up. Unacceptable!

It seems that there is just a small percentage of kids doing chores these days. A survey conducted by Braun Research found that 82 percent of adults reported doing chores as a child but only 28 percent were having their own children do household chores.

Considering that doing chores is shown to have positive impacts on children, this is an astounding statistic. "Childhood chores lead to increased competence with necessary life skills, an increase in instilling values, and even general well-being. Chores and housework are linked to happiness in children as they feel they are making meaningful contributions to their families."

As a result of no chores, it appears more children are showing signs of entitlement. This shows up in ways such as learned helplessness, whining about doing any kind of work, and a sense that the world revolves around them.

Now, I'm not saying that if children don't have chores they are doomed, but I do feel that chores offer them many developmental benefits.

There are many resources you can find online regarding appropriate chores for different age levels. Believe it or not, simple chores can begin as early as 2 years of age!

PARENT ACTION PLAN: Have your children and teens do chores for no money. Express gratitude and show them that their kindness will be reciprocated by another act of kindness.

CHILD'S LESSON LEARNED: Kindness begets kindness. I like doing things for others because it makes me feel good, and that kind of energy comes back to me.

DON'T HIDE BEHIND
DEVICES

There are so many opportunities to communicate with your teens, but far too often I see those chances obliterated by both parents and teens. One of my favorite times to have conversations is in the car, especially to and from school.

This is when I find out so many things about school, their teachers, and their friends. On the way to school, we talk about what we're looking forward to (or not looking forward to). On the way home, we give wrap-ups of the day.

Again, this should start at an early age. My son used to give me one-word answers, but after years of questioning and talking in the car, he now gives me full reports of his day. Sometimes it just takes persistence and a little bit of encouragement.

My 22-year-old daughter just told me recently how much she misses our car talks from those days. She lives on the other side of the country, so we don't have that opportunity anymore, but our communication is still rock solid. Ironically, our main form of communication now is texting, but she still comes to me for advice and wants to get my input on things.

Another great opening for interaction is during meals. I have always had a no-device rule at the table. How can children learn social skills by eating and hiding behind a screen?

What shocks me is when I see adults doing this! You're *showing* your children that whatever is on your screen is more important than being with them. This may not be your intention, but this is what you're modeling.

How in the world did we survive before smartphones? We learned that things *can wait*! Sometimes we get caught up in the notion that there must be an immediate response to everything. I think we all need to take a collective breath and realize that, unless something is an immediate life or death matter, *it can wait*!

Restaurants are another place where there is an opportunity to teach our kids the importance of socializing without devices. It upsets me when I see a family at dinner with their teens, not only on devices but wearing earbuds! They're allowed to completely tune out their family at the dinner table? No way. This should not be happening.

I always chuckle when I see a group of teens at a restaurant, and they are *all* on their phones. You may want to tell your teen about a fun game called phone stacking. At the beginning of the meal, have everyone stack their phone in the middle of the table, and the first person to look at their phone has to pay for the meal!

The dinner table is for eye contact, conversation, and etiquette. What are we teaching our kids by ignoring these very essential life lessons?

Socializing is something that takes practice, and without it, you are doing a great disservice to your children and teens. They will have a difficult time at social gatherings and interviews, and they will not learn how to instigate or engage in conversations.

Hiding behind devices is a crutch for those with social anxiety and can sometimes be purposefully used to avoid interaction.

There is scientific research behind the importance of good dinner etiquette, too. "Studies have shown that young children may be more prone to fussy eating and other negative behaviors when there are more distractions at meals," said Saltzman, a postdoctoral research fellow with Harvard University's T. H. Chan School of Public Health and the Massachusetts General Hospital for Children Department of Academic Pediatrics. "Parents can consider removing toys, pets, and other distractions so that young children are focused on the meal and parents have more opportunities to encourage healthy eating habits."

The important thing to remember is, in order to enforce it, you need to model it as well.

PARENT ACTION PLAN: Limit the amount of digital device time in your car and restrict it at the table during meals.

CHILD'S LESSON LEARNED: I will learn important social skills that will take me far in life. I will learn to respect other people and show them I care by being present.

TEACH COMPASSION AND EMPATHY

I fully believe we currently have a compassion crisis going on in the world. I see children who laugh at other people's pain and kids who don't see how their actions affect others. Bullying, taunting, making fun of, mocking, the list goes on and on.

And the worst part is we're seeing it from adult leaders and people who are supposed to be role models.

Compassion and empathy are traits that should be modeled at home. We need to take the time to show our children that we should care about others, that there is suffering out there, and how our negative behavior can have a harmful impact on others.

As a teacher, there have been many times that I've been shocked by the lack of empathy some of my students have. It's as if they have no ability to see things from others' perspectives. They've said things to me that shows me they have a narrow view of people.

For instance, I always broach the topic of homelessness during class because it has to do with a story that we've read. Inevitably, I will have a few students tell me homeless people are "dumb or lazy." When I discuss mental illness, financial hardships, and physical disabilities, it's like a door opens in their mind that they never considered before. Then, I show them videos of homeless people who were once professors or talented musicians and how they became homeless, and their heart opens up to other possibilities besides homeless people being "dumb and lazy."

I always try my hardest to show these children why it's important to be compassionate. Some get it and some don't. Most of the time, the ones who don't get it are the ones who are left on devices most of the time, not monitored at home, and don't have a good honest relationship with their parents.

Parents, I know you're tired. I know you're frustrated. But if you don't put in the time and effort with your children at a young age to raise loving, caring adults, it will backfire on you. If we want to see a change in our local, state, national, and global communities, we cannot raise a generation of selfish, unempathetic people.

Narrow-minded thinking will be our downfall if we don't instill empathy to future generations. Selfishness and entitlement are negative by-products of indifference.

It is not just me who sees the erosion of empathy in our society. An article in the *Atlantic* states: "Perhaps we shouldn't be surprised, then, that kindness appears to be in decline. A rigorous analysis of annual surveys of American college students showed a substantial drop from 1979 to 2009 in empathy and in imagining the perspectives of others. Over this period, students grew less likely to feel concerned for people less fortunate than themselves—and less bothered by seeing others treated unfairly."

As this article also states, parents can sometimes focus too much on grades, test results, game scores, and awards rather than kindness, compassion, and emotional availability. We need to be careful about what we're putting our attention on with our children. If we center on the wrong things, those are the things our children will undoubtedly focus on to get your approval.

Also, too many teens live in a "bubble" of existence. What I mean by this is that they are used to their life of easy convenience—food on the table, clothes on their back, technology at their fingertips, access to quality education, and so forth. They should go outside their "bubble" and see how other people live. Volunteering at senior centers and homeless shelters might be a start. Look into other ways your child can see a world beyond their own and how what we do can affect others.

Show them to care for living creatures and to be involved in environmental causes. These types of engagements can illustrate how our actions impact the world.

PARENT ACTION PLAN: Instill compassion by having your teen do community service. You can even make it something you do together. If this is not possible, engage in content like videos, movies, and books about other people's hardships, and TALK to them about it.

CHILD'S LESSON LEARNED: There is more out there than just me. Other people and animals are struggling or hurting, and I can try to understand their battles and pain.

IF YOU MESS UP, APOLOGIZE!

There's nothing worse than not taking ownership of your own mistakes. This is a trait that needs to be demonstrated by you.

Acting as if you're superhuman and incapable of having faults builds a level of distrust with your child.

They will see right through you and peg you as a liar and someone who is a bully. This can lead to issues with defiance and dishonesty. How are they expected to trust you if you blatantly lie about responsibility?

It's important to be authentic and vulnerable with your child.

In the past, a lot of parents believed that exposing any kind of vulnerability would mean showing weakness to their child and that it would ultimately have a negative impact on their relationship. My own mother grew up in a patriarchal household during the 1930-50s where her father had ultimate power and saw showing emotion as a sign of weakness. There was no room for mistakes, openness, or nurturing because he was so closed off. He yelled and was always in control, no matter how irrational his demands were.

Many parents believed weakness would create an unbalanced relationship where the child didn't respect their parent, and the child would have more power over the parent. This couldn't be further from the truth.

Parents also thought that children who showed weakness would turn into helpless adults. As a teacher, I always wondered why so many children tried to stifle their tears or ran away when they were hurt. They were told at a young age "Don't cry." "Wipe those tears." "Be tough."

This needs to change. Children need to understand that all emotions are valid, and they need coping skills to navigate through them. One of the ways they can do that is to watch you apologize in a positive and meaningful way.

Once there is no longer stigma attached to apologizing, it will be easy for your child to apologize in their own interactions with family and peers.

PARENT ACTION PLAN: When you make a mistake, own up to it, apologize, and explain how you will work on correcting that behavior.

CHILD'S LESSON LEARNED: My parents are honest and genuine and respect my feelings. There is no shame in apologizing, and I will also take ownership when I make a mistake with others.

CHAPTER

6

GRATITUDE IS A GREAT ATTITUDE

The more grateful you are, the more you have to be grateful for. Teach your child this at a young age. Develop a plan to show gratitude in their lives.

One thing my mom always taught me when I thought the world was crashing down on me was that there are others who are suffering way more than me. Be appreciative of the things you do have—a roof over your head, good health, family, and so forth. When you focus on the good, you will find more goodness in your life.

That's not to say you can't feel your hurt or your pain. Just don't stay there. Remember that each moment in your life is just a moment, not your whole life.

Remind yourself of all the things you have to be thankful for. This sets your child up for ways to cope with pain in the future.

Find examples of people who have very little but are grateful for what they have. Show them what true suffering is. Read historical texts about other people.

According to Harvard Medical School's website, "Gratitude helps people feel more positive emotions, relish good experiences, improve their health, deal with adversity, and build strong relationships."

The overlying goal is to teach your child to go outside of themselves. Growing up is a very self-centered time, and it can feel as if the whole world revolves around you.

Don't you remember your teen angst? The drama that ensued with either cliques, gossip, or unrequited love? If children don't develop coping mechanisms, this can lead to many problems in the future such as depression and cynicism.

I am finding more of my students dealing with depression at younger ages. My concern is that these children are left on devices most of the time and navigate them on their own. I will discuss more of this later.

PARENT ACTION PLAN: Create a way to model gratitude. Have a gratitude jar and write one thing down that you're grateful for. Or give your child a gratitude journal.

CHILD'S LESSON LEARNED: I have so many wonderful things in my life to be grateful for. My pain or hurt is only temporary.

GROWTH MINDSET > FIXED MINDSET

The growth mindset starts at home. This mindset empowers children and creates ways for them to grow and mature. A fixed mindset will never lead to progress. It's limiting and self-defeating.

So, what's the difference between the two?

A growth mindset is knowing how to turn weaknesses into strengths, believing there is always a lesson to be learned, understanding that giving effort leads to success, seeing setbacks as part of the process, and finding feedback essential to personal growth.

A fixed mindset is thinking weaknesses cannot be changed, giving up learning, seeing setbacks as a reason to quit, and finding feedback insulting and pointless.

There is a possibility to educate your child on a growth mindset in so many situations—while watching TV, working on homework, sitting at the dinner table, riding in the car, going on a bike ride, or a hike—the list goes on and on. Don't miss out on those opportunities whenever they are presented to you.

How do you teach a growth mindset? It's important to first explain what the differences are between the two and how different the sets of thinking are. When tough situations inevitably arise, these are perfect openings for you to explain how a growth mindset's perspective will get better results.

For instance, consider your reaction if your child got a bad grade on a test they studied for, gets angry, and says what's the point of studying. This is an opening for you to sit down and discuss how failure isn't an ending. It's an opportunity to reflect and learn from it. You can ask "Why did you get a low score? How could you have studied differently?" Then, have your child come up with an action plan. This teaches your child that they have control over any obstacles they may encounter along their life journey.

According to a Chilean study mentioned in the Mindset Scholar Network, researchers found that among 10th graders, "students who held a growth mindset were three times more likely to score in the top 20% on the test, while students with a fixed mindset were four times more likely to score in the bottom 20%."

People with growth mindsets are more successful and more resilient. They value and see learning in failure. They understand that their perspectives can change over time by gaining new information. They don't take challenging discussions personally and engage in thoughtful dialogue without losing their temper.

This also lends itself to *grit*. This refers to having the persistence to push through any stumbling blocks you may encounter. Gritty people understand that with success comes failure and with growth comes setbacks, which are just a part of the journey, not the destination.

A great book to understand this is Angela Duckworth's *Grit: The Power of Passion and Perseverance*. This book explains why some people with less talent can achieve more than those with more natural abilities.

These behaviors are learned from you. Do you show courage in the face of difficulty or freak out when times get tough? Are you persistent when faced with a daunting task, or do you give up easily?

PARENT ACTION PLAN: Discuss the difference between both growth and fixed mindsets on a regular basis. Print out a chart and put it on the refrigerator as a reference. When difficult things happen, talk about what can be learned from the situation.

CHILD'S LESSON LEARNED: I have the power to change how I feel. I grow through what I go through and there's always something to learn from every situation—no matter how good or bad.

PART 2:

Education

BE INVOLVED—BUT NOT TOO INVOLVED!

There is a fine line here, and as a teacher, I'm hyper-aware of it. We definitely want parents to be involved in their children's education by showing up to back-to-school nights, chaperoning trips, responding to teacher emails, and so forth. But there's a boundary that gets crossed too many times. The term "helicopter parents" comes to mind when discussing this.

You have to understand that we teachers give class-work assignments that show us your child's competencies. We know their vocabulary level, artistic strengths, creative ability, and academic proficiency.

So, when our students have a 6th or 7th-grade competency and come in with a project completed at a 12th-grade level, we know that they are not the only ones doing their homework. In fact, they may not be doing it at all. Science fair, anyone?

How is this teaching your child independence? In elementary school, I understand wanting to lend a hand to your child, but in middle school, you need to be as hands-free as possible when it comes to doing their work. It doesn't mean you can't help them, but don't do their work for them.

They need to learn how to be resourceful. They need to understand *how* to make improvements and aim higher.

As a perfectionist, I realize that sometimes it's difficult to allow your child to turn in something that isn't how you would have done it. I remember that when my son completed his 6th-grade science fair project I cringed on the inside when I saw his final product, because it wasn't "perfect." The lettering and symmetry were off and some of the construction paper was cut sloppily, but I was so proud that it was 100 percent his own work. To me, that was the most important aspect of this experience. I wanted him to know what hard work was and to earn his grade by himself.

The next year, when he completed his 7th-grade science fair project on his own, his end product floored me! He said he learned how to perfect it after seeing other examples from the year before. He learned his own lesson and applied it in real life.

Isn't that what education is all about? My son saw other students' projects and took a mental note of how he wanted to improve his project the next year. What a learning experience for him!

A 2019 study from Florida State University found that "kids who had helicopter parents were more likely to experience burnout from schoolwork, and they had a harder time transitioning from school to the real world."

Parents may be too involved because they want to help their child, but the irony is that they are essentially hindering their growth. I've had students who had helicopter parents and then couldn't make it when they went away to college. They had no skills to manage life on their own and would soon return.

Remember, parents, the goal is to assist your child in learning to fly on their own. The goal is *not* to rely on you for the rest of their lives. You want them to be able to make decisions on their own, but they cannot do that if you are constantly making the decisions for them.

Our problem as parents is that we want them to avoid making mistakes, but sometimes that is the only way they will learn.

I know it's difficult at times to see your child make a mistake or fail, but it's the only way they will be able to become fully independent, functioning adults.

PARENT ACTION PLAN: Make a conscious effort to have your teen do their own work 100 percent of the time. Stop stunting their growth.

CHILD'S LEARNED LESSON: I am independent and can figure out how to get things done on my own. I've learned how to be resourceful even if I'm unsure about something.

IF THEY ARE
STRUGGLING—HELP!

Now you may be scratching your head because I just explained how you should be hands-off with your child, but now I'm telling you to *help*! This is only if you are receiving emails from teachers, seeing that their grades are dropping, and/or noticing that they seem to be living inside themselves.

If your child is truly struggling, you need to step in and provide the resources necessary—sometimes it's counseling, testing, actively checking that homework is completed, medication (as a final resource), or something else.

I know medication can be a touchy subject, and I completely understand that, but sometimes it is necessary. I have seen some of my students make a drastic turn-around for the better because they received medication, and their parents were on top of it.

Many times, I've recognized when a student hadn't taken their medication or when they needed to up their dosage because they had a growth spurt.

I am by no means saying that medication is the answer, but if it is for your child, then you need to follow up with it and make sure they are taking it and that someone is monitoring dosages as they grow.

I also see signs of depression and low self-esteem in some of my students, and if a teacher or counselor reaches out to you about it, it is necessary to figure this out ASAP with a licensed expert. There is absolutely no shame in depression and anxiety, but it should be dealt with head-on and immediately.

Also, some children are born to fly sooner than others. I have middle school students who are 100 percent self-sufficient, but there are many who are not, and if parents don't step in to help, they will flounder.

Tools like organization, planning, and follow-through need to be instilled *at home*. Nothing makes me scratch my head more than when a parent asks *why* their child isn't doing their homework. A teacher can only do so much.

An article summarizing research about parent involvement states, "No matter their income or background, students with involved parents are more likely to have higher grades and test scores, attend school regularly, have better social skills, show improved behavior, and adapt well to school."

With today's technology, gradebooks are digital. Parents have no excuse for not knowing their children's grades and assignments.

I should also mention that we teachers are human. There may be times where the assignments are not updated or there's a mistake in the gradebook. This is why we remind students to write the assignments down in an old school or digital agenda of some sort. This is not only a great habit to instill, but it will guarantee they know the assignments in case (1) the teacher didn't update the online component or (2) the gradebook site is down (which happens!).

Again, children need to understand that they need to take the initiative when it comes to their own schoolwork.

PARENT ACTION PLAN: Check their grades, check in with teachers, and keep that line of communication open, but don't DO the work for them.

CHILD'S LESSON LEARNED: My parents really care about me and my well-being. I feel loved.

CHAPTER

10

PARTNER WITH TEACHERS

I think I can speak for all teachers when I say we *want* your teen to succeed. We don't have some hidden agenda, and we're certainly not "out" for your child.

However, I must tell you something that you may not want to hear. Your child will lie to you.

I know, I know—GASP! I don't care how great your child is; there will come a time that your teen will lie to you to either cover for themselves or for their friend.

This is why I am always dumbfounded when I contact a parent about their child's behavior, and I get a parent reply like, "Well, Johnny says that's not true." This doesn't happen often, but it has happened enough for me to shake my head in wonderment.

If a teacher contacts you about anything, please be supportive.

A CNBC article examined the challenges teachers face: "PDK International, a professional association for educators, polled 2,389 American adults, including 1,083 parents of school-age children and 556 public school teachers . . . 50% of those 556 teachers say they have considered leaving the profession. In addition to low pay and stress, teachers found the lack of respect they received as another reason they wanted to leave the teaching profession."

On top of planning lessons, grading, contacting other parents, attending staff meetings, and managing my own life at home with my kids, I assure you that I am not making up a story about your child. Can there be a misunderstanding or miscommunication? Of course!

However, if you have a good relationship with the teachers, these hiccups will be few and far between.

If you do have an issue with a teacher, be discreet about it. Don't talk negatively about the teacher in front of your child. Meet with the teacher or administration privately. Often, a face-to-face meeting can clear the air.

When you talk disparagingly about the teacher in front of your child, you are showing your child that they can disrespect the teacher too. This can lead to a lot more problems down the road with defiant and insolent behavior.

PARENT ACTION PLAN: Send an email to your child's teachers, saying that you look forward to part-

nering with them, and if there's anything they need, feel free to email you any time.

CHILD'S LESSON LEARNED: My parents respect my teachers and have a good line of communication with them.

SCHOOL IS A PRIORITY AND A PRIVILEGE

As a child and teen, I had perfect attendance. Not because I was forced to go to school, but I inherently *hated* missing school. I was afraid I would miss something extremely important and would get behind in my studies. I had a severe case of FOMO (fear of missing out)!

I guess since I was so entrenched in my own teen drama, I never noticed other students' absences so much. Unless it was my best friend or the boy I had a crush on.

When I became a teacher, I felt like I entered the twilight zone. I had students missing weeks of school because of extended vacations (some right after a 2-week holiday), going to theme parks, and missing classes for haircuts, manicures, and pedicures. I had some students extending their summers for as long as a month!

A year ago, I took my youngest son to Disneyland on a school day, but it was because we were gifted free tickets, and we could only use them during the week. The summer days were blocked off, so that wasn't a choice.

He was so upset and didn't want to go. He's a conscientious student and inherited my FOMO at school DNA, but I explained that this would never happen again, and these circumstances were out of my control.

So, yes, I get that things happen. But I'm also saying if it does, explain why, and then don't make it habitual.

Because think about the message you're sending your child: *School isn't a priority. You can miss it for pretty much any reason.*

Here is the problem with that mindset. It becomes customary. They then become overwhelmed with the amount of work they must make up, and as a result, they start to lag with what is going on in the class. This makes them want to miss more school to "catch up," which then creates a vicious cycle.

I also believe that if this is done regularly, their work ethic will weaken. How will this translate into college and the workforce? What you show them as being priorities as a youth will greatly impact them as adults.

A child missing two days a month can be considered chronically absent. Keep track of their absences because it may not seem like a lot when missed days are spread out, but those days quickly add up.

There are many negative statistics that correlate with absenteeism, and it starts from an early age. It can negatively impact reading proficiency and overall academic performance. Believe it or not, by 6th grade, chronic absenteeism can indicate a higher chance of dropping out of high school.

Also, be careful of teens using illness as avoidance. I see this frequently as well. I've had students mysteriously only get sick on test days, project due days, and presentation days.

If a teacher reaches out to you because they're seeing a pattern, try to find out from your child what is really going on. There can be social anxiety, a negative relationship with a friend, bullying, or academic struggles.

They can't call in sick at work because they don't want to be there for their presentation in front of the CEO.

One thing I've always told my students and my own children is that school is the most important job they have right now. Everything else is secondary.

If your child has never read the story of Malala Yousafzai, then they should add it to their reading list (there is a young adult version).

Malala's story shows how much education is valued, but how difficult it was for her to access as a young girl in Taliban-run northwest Pakistan. This story is eye-opening. We take our education for granted in the United States and have no genuine appreciation for how important it is to our foundation.

Consider this: "According to data from the UNESCO Institute for Statistics (UIS), about 263 million children, adolescents, and youth worldwide (or one in every five) are out of school."

This is a striking statistic since we know that in the United States, education is an essential component of a child's development.

I also think sometimes our parenting plays into how our children view education. Sometimes teachers are disrespected. School is seen as something that is easily missed.

Of course, I don't speak for all parents, but I've seen a lot of this happening. I've had interesting experiences where I'm at birthday parties or sporting events and other parents don't know I'm a teacher in the school, and I hear what they say.

Inevitably, they're embarrassed when they find out I'm a teacher, but my point remains. There are some disgruntled parents out there who feel comfortable voicing their negative opinions in front of other parents and their own children. I wonder if their energy would be better served in making education a positive experience for their child, instead of miserable for the teacher or school.

I wish parents could see what teachers go through on a daily basis. I wonder how their perspective would change.

Now I'm not saying you can't speak your mind and want a change in your child's education, but I think it's important to keep those conversations private and with administrators only. Talking badly about the school, teachers, and administration in front of your child does not show respect to the educators or to their education.

Disrespecting teachers and the education system does not help your child foster a love for learning.

If you're excited about learning and education, it will trickle down to them. It's the same principle I apply as a teacher. If I want my students to be passionate about learning, I need to be enthusiastic about how I teach my content.

If you show your child that you respect their teacher, they will too. Remind them how lucky they are to attend school and have access to school supplies. That's not the case in many underdeveloped countries.

Bring that attitude of gratitude into their education.

PARENT ACTION PLAN: Reinforce the rule that only special occasions or circumstances warrant missing school. Do not voice negative opinions about school in front of your teen. Discuss how, in some countries, going to school is considered a luxury only allowed to a very small population.

CHILD'S LESSON LEARNED: School is important, and I don't want to miss anything. My parents respect my school, my teachers, and my administrators. I am lucky to be able to get an education.

CHAPTER

12

INTEGRITY IS A MUST

One thing I've noticed throughout my teaching career is how cheating and lying have become rampant. Even the so-called "good" kids are doing it. It's as if honesty is not even an option—it's all about saving face.

Most teens don't realize that we already know the truth before we ask them for it. We hope, that when confronted, they will choose honesty. Unfortunately, a lot of times they won't.

What makes it worse for me is when they keep arguing about it. They do not want to relent.

Why has lying become so easy? I've heard pretty much every excuse in the book. According to some of my students, their iPads or computers just mysteriously delete everything or lose documents. Websites that record time-stamped assignments are wrong. They had no idea they even had homework. I could go on and on, but it's always disheartening to me.

I try to explain that I would rather be disappointed with the truth than lied to my face. It's so much more difficult to earn back trust than it is to get over the disappointment of a bad choice.

Plagiarism is also widespread. With the surge of website research, it is all too easy for students to simply copy and paste and call it their own work. Thank goodness for websites like Turnitin.com that can show teachers and the students where it is copied from.

Students cheating on homework, quizzes, and tests has also become a problem. And I'm just talking from a teacher's perspective at school.

Research backs me up on these observations: "In a survey of 24,000, students at 70 high schools, Donald McCabe (Rutgers University) found that 64 percent of students admitted to cheating on a test, 58 percent admitted to plagiarism, and 95 percent said they participated in some form of cheating, whether it was on a test, plagiarism or copying homework."

These statistics are shocking. The rise of the Internet has been a contributing factor to this dilemma as plagiarism is as easy as a copy and paste. I don't remember this kind of rampant plagiarism before the rise of the Internet.

Parents, I know we see this dishonesty at home as well.

What makes a child want to lie before telling the truth?

We need to model the behavior. We can't expect our children to understand the value of integrity if we don't demonstrate it in front of them. It's necessary to show them that doing the right thing is not always the easy thing. It's also important to do the right thing, even when no one is watching.

If I find money, I return it. If I find someone's keys or wallet, I turn it in to authorities. I've stopped to help someone in a car accident.

We can watch TV shows or movies with our children and discuss how easy things would have been if the character had simply told the truth from the beginning.

With characters and real-life role models (ranging from Charlie Brown to Malala) who act honestly and ethically, kids can learn the value of telling the truth, acting sincerely, treating people equally, and taking responsibility for their actions.

It also goes back to what I discussed in the first section of chapter 1. If a young child is honest with you about breaking something, and you react by yelling and being scary, do you really think they'll want to tell the truth or open up to you in the future?

Don't get me wrong; there should be consequences for negative behavior, but the *way* in which you give that consequence can be the difference between your child feeling safe or unsafe with you.

I know it's impossible to keep your child from lying. Sometimes it happens to test out the behavior, seek attention, or avoid hurting someone else's feelings. However, persistent issues of lying and/or cheating are grounds for concern.

PARENT ACTION PLAN: Find shows or movies that you can watch together to discuss integrity and honesty with your child. Give them certain situations and practice the best ways to handle them. Show them that hard work is honored.

CHILD'S LESSON LEARNED: I know how to handle difficult situations, and when I feel the need to lie, I know it is ultimately hurting myself and those I care about.

PART 3:

The Digital World

WHAT AGE SHOULD I GIVE MY CHILD A PHONE?

Before I delve in any further, I want to note that I am not anti-technology. In fact, as I mentioned earlier, I love it. Even though I'm a digital immigrant, I embraced the digital world with open arms 20 years ago and have learned so much since then.

Technology has allowed us to be a global community, to interact with more people than usual, and to learn valuable lessons. As an educator, I use digital platforms to teach my subject matter and love how I can individualize lessons and engage my students. I am constantly trying to keep up with the ever-changing world of technology as I appreciate its many benefits.

With that being said, I believe that common sense goes a long way. Children cannot be expected to use technology without parameters on their usage, starting with smartphones.

Remember, smartphones allow your child to have access to a world of adult content right at their fingertips.

In my opinion, a child under the age of 13 doesn't need to have a smartphone with access to Wi-Fi and social media. However, I am startled by the statistics suggesting that other parents differ in their views on this topic.

According to NPR, "Just over half of children in the United States—53 percent—now own a smartphone by the age of 11. And 84 percent of teenagers now have their own phones, immersing themselves in a rich and complex world of experiences that adults sometimes need a lot of decoding to understand."

Through my research, I have found some people draw the line for a phone at 16. Bill Gates, a co-founder of Microsoft, says he didn't give his children phones until they were 14. Clearly, it's up to the parents' discretion, but the bottom line should be your child's maturity and responsibility levels. Can your child be responsible with such an expensive gadget? Are they already doing well with in-person communication? Will they be able to adhere to screen-time limits? Can they be trusted with not taking or sharing embarrassing or inappropriate photos? Are they doing well in school? These are just some of the questions you should be asking yourself before making a decision.

If you feel they need a way to connect with you, you can invest in a simple phone that only allows texting and phone calls. Kids VTech and Jitterbug are among many companies that produce these types of phones. It doesn't take more than a quick online search or conversation with someone in a tech store to find out your options.

Please don't feel the rush to buy an iPhone or Android for a small child. I wonder why parents seem to be in a rush to give their child a phone. Do they feel their child will be left out if they don't have one? They won't be liked, or they won't be popular? Think about *why* before taking the leap.

My children always tried to get me to buy them a phone before they reached 13, and they loved to tell me, "All my other friends have them." My reply, "Good for them!" It can really be as simple as that.

They got so tired of hearing that response that they eventually gave up. They knew I wouldn't budge.

When you give a child a smartphone, you are opening up a world of temptation and danger. Don't believe me? Talk to your local police department's sex crime unit. Or even easier—read the daily news. There isn't a day that goes by where we don't hear about a deranged adult trying to meet a minor they met through social media.

Fortunately, police detectives who pose as minors online are catching a lot of these criminals, but there are so many out there—it's impossible to catch them all.

My two eldest, who are now in their 20s, continue to thank me for taking such a "hard-line" about the phone situation. They said nothing good would have come from them having a phone so early.

And it's not just about online safety, but it's also about body image, self-esteem, and online bullying (which I will discuss later on in the book).

PARENT ACTION PLAN: No smartphones until 13 (or older).

CHILD'S LESSON LEARNED: My parents care about my safety and well-being. I need to show my parents that I am responsible and mature enough to own a smartphone.

NO ELECTRONICS IN THE BEDROOM

I can't begin to tell you how many times I have associated poor grades, lack of sleep, and inattention in the classroom with one of my students having a computer and/or a TV in their bedroom.

It's usually one of the first things I ask when I'm in a parent conference regarding a student's declining grades.

"Where does Sally do her schoolwork?"

More often than not, the parent will reply, "In her bedroom."

"Do you know if Sally is actually doing her homework?"

"Well, no, she closes the door, but she tells me she's doing it."

Herein lies the problem.

Do you really think your child is doing their work behind closed doors with the whole world of the Internet and games at their fingertips?

If you do, you are in serious denial, my friend.

I don't care how "good" your child is; this is a recipe for disaster.

My children never had computers or TVs in their bedrooms until their senior year of high school. Not only that, their devices had to be turned into me every single night. Because again, do you think they're not on their phones, computers, TVs, or video game consoles all night long? It's likely that with access to these electronic distractions they are texting their friends, zombie watching TikTok videos, binge-watching Netflix, or playing Fortnite.

When I was a teenager and had a phone in my room, I remember talking on the phone until all hours of the night, and I was an honor student! I also remember at one point putting a stop to it, because it was affecting my performance in school and my extracurricular activities. I was prone to migraines, and I was sure they were heightened from lack of sleep.

Parents, we must do better! We can't be so complacent and think our children will never do anything wrong. It is up to us to set boundaries and guidelines for them.

Yes, your children are going to whine and complain. They may get angry with you. It doesn't matter. Be firm and show them that you love and care about them so much that you want to protect them by taking away their devices at night. I understand it's difficult not to give into them, but remember, you are a parent. Your job is to help them navigate the world in a safe space.

They will sleep better. They will feel better about themselves. They will do better in school.

Shockingly, most parents are not being proactive in setting boundaries for electronics. "Almost 72 percent of young people between 6 and 17 years old have at least one electronic device in their bedroom, according to a National Sleep Foundation survey. Kids who leave these devices on during the night sleep up to one hour less on average each night, the group found."

Sleep is important to the physical and mental development of kids and teens, and from what I see in the classroom, students are not getting enough. They are dragging into school disinterested, unfocused, and forgetful. I know those are common traits in teenagers, but when I hear them talk about how little sleep they got the night before, I know that these behaviors are exacerbated by their sleep patterns, and I suspect digital devices may be at play.

Science backs me up on the importance of teens getting enough sleep: "Research says that teens need between 8-10 hours of sleep at night to function well at school and for positive health results. Less than that can show a decrease in academic performance, mood swings, and even adverse health effects."

Lack of sleep weakens the immune system and can have devastating effects on teens who begin driving, as sleepiness is a major cause of auto accidents. "The National Highway Traffic Safety Administration estimates that drowsy driving was responsible for 72,000 crashes, 44,000 injuries, and 800 deaths in 2013. However, these numbers are underestimated, and up to 6,000 fatal crashes each year may be caused by drowsy drivers."

The research is crystal clear. Children's bedrooms should be a sanctuary for rest and relaxation. Get them used to reading or doing some other low stimulation activity before bedtime. Looking at bright screens at night directly affects their circadian rhythm (biological clock for sleep) and suppresses the secretion of melatonin (a hormone that regulates the sleep-wake cycle).

The ultimate goal is to ensure that your children have healthy sleep patterns that carry them into adulthood.

PARENT ACTION PLAN: No electronics in the bedroom. Confiscate any mobile devices (laptops, iPads, tablets, phones, etc.) every single night.

CHILD'S LESSON LEARNED: My parents care enough about me to set limits. Even though it's annoying, I know they're doing it because they love me.

WHOSE PROPERTY IS IT?

I can't begin to tell you how many times I have associated poor grades, lack of sleep, and inattention in the classroom with one of my students having a computer and/or a TV in their bedroom.

It's usually one of the first things I ask when I'm in a parent conference regarding a student's declining grades.

"Where does Sally do her schoolwork?"

More often than not, the parent will reply, "In her bedroom."

"Do you know if Sally is actually doing her homework?"

"Well, no, she closes the door, but she tells me she's doing it."

Herein lies the problem.

Do you really think your child is doing their work behind closed doors with the whole world of the Internet and games at their fingertips?

If you do, you are in serious denial, my friend.

I don't care how "good" your child is; this is a recipe for disaster.

My children never had computers or TVs in their bedrooms until their senior year of high school. Not only that, their devices had to be turned into me every single night. Because again, do you think they're not on their phones, computers, TVs, or video game consoles all night long? It's likely that with access to these electronic distractions they are texting their friends, zombie watching TikTok videos, binge-watching Netflix, or playing Fortnite.

When I was a teenager and had a phone in my room, I remember talking on the phone until all hours of the night, and I was an honor student! I also remember at one point putting a stop to it, because it was affecting my performance in school and my extracurricular activities. I was prone to migraines, and I was sure they were heightened from lack of sleep.

Parents, we must do better! We can't be so complacent and think our children will never do anything wrong. It is up to us to set boundaries and guidelines for them.

Yes, your children are going to whine and complain. They may get angry with you. It doesn't matter. Be firm and show them that you love and care about them so much that you want to protect them by taking away their devices at night. I understand it's difficult not to give into them, but remember, you are a parent. Your job is to help them navigate the world in a safe space.

They will sleep better. They will feel better about themselves. They will do better in school.

Shockingly, most parents are not being proactive in setting boundaries for electronics. "Almost 72 percent of young people between 6 and 17 years old have at least one electronic device in their bedroom, according to a National Sleep Foundation survey. Kids who leave these devices on during the night sleep up to one hour less on average each night, the group found."

Sleep is important to the physical and mental development of kids and teens, and from what I see in the classroom, students are not getting enough. They are dragging into school disinterested, unfocused, and forgetful. I know those are common traits in teenagers, but when I hear them talk about how little sleep they got the night before, I know that these behaviors are exacerbated by their sleep patterns, and I suspect digital devices may be at play.

Science backs me up on the importance of teens getting enough sleep: "Research says that teens need between 8-10 hours of sleep at night to function well at school and for positive health results. Less than that can show a decrease in academic performance, mood swings, and even adverse health effects."

Lack of sleep weakens the immune system and can have devastating effects on teens who begin driving, as sleepiness is a major cause of auto accidents. "The National Highway Traffic Safety Administration estimates that drowsy driving was responsible for 72,000 crashes, 44,000 injuries, and 800 deaths in 2013. However, these numbers are underestimated, and up to 6,000 fatal crashes each year may be caused by drowsy drivers."

The research is crystal clear. Children's bedrooms should be a sanctuary for rest and relaxation. Get them used to reading or doing some other low stimulation activity before bedtime. Looking at bright screens at night directly affects their circadian rhythm (biological clock for sleep) and suppresses the secretion of melatonin (a hormone that regulates the sleep-wake cycle).

The ultimate goal is to ensure that your children have healthy sleep patterns that carry them into adulthood.

PARENT ACTION PLAN: No electronics in the bedroom. Confiscate any mobile devices (laptops, iPads, tablets, phones, etc.) every single night.

CHILD'S LESSON LEARNED: My parents care enough about me to set limits. Even though it's annoying, I know they're doing it because they love me.

DIGITAL ADDICTION IS ON THE RISE

Believe it or not, digital addiction is a real problem for many teens and adults. There have been multiple studies on teens addicted to the screen, and it starts early.

According to a recent study completed by the University of Hong Kong, 6 percent of those around the globe have an Internet addiction. With only 39 percent of the world having access to the Internet, that is an alarming statistic.

I have had students who physically struggle with *not* being on an electronic device, and if they're on it, they have a difficult time keeping their work academic-based. They start opening up tabs, checking emails, messaging, playing games, and so forth. I've had students break down in front of me and tell me that they know it's wrong but confess that they struggle with self-control.

This is not surprising, because the area of the brain known as the prefrontal cortex doesn't fully develop until after adolescence. This area of the brain is in charge of things like self-control, planning, organization, and memory. This may also explain the forgetfulness in teens!

Since the prefrontal cortex of teens is not fully developed, they cannot set guidelines for themselves and need us to do it for them.

The Center for Parenting Education states, "It's estimated that kids and teens between the ages of 8 to 28 spend about 44.5 hours each week in front of digital screens. About 23% of kids and teens have reported that they actually feel as if they have addictions to video games. That breaks down to 31% of males and 13% of females."

I can't stress this enough: *Children need you to set the guidelines. Don't put your guard down when it comes to technology.* They will surprise you when they have access to other things besides going down the rabbit hole of the Internet or playing video games. They can read, bike, swim, run, draw, be creative, play an instrument, or just relax. Mindful moments are underrated.

I get it. We're tired. We're overwhelmed. We just want time for ourselves. But technology is numbing everyone and is causing a serious communication breakdown in the family unit. Our children are becoming digital zombies, and unfortunately, a lot of us are allowing it to happen right before our eyes.

If they are doing homework, reading, or studying, it might be helpful to take the phone away, so they are not distracted by the constant notifications and the temptation of doing something else.

The Pew Research Center states: "Fully 72% of teens say they often or sometimes check for messages or notifications as soon as they wake up, while roughly four-in-ten say they feel anxious when they do not have their cellphone with them. Overall, 56% of teens associate the absence of their cellphone with at least one of these three emotions: loneliness, being upset, or feeling anxious."

However, you need to set an example. You can't be preaching about the overuse of devices when you are on yours constantly.

I've seen parents so preoccupied with their phones they don't even see their toddlers running away from them or crossing the street. It's quite frightening!

The Pew Research Center discusses this as well: "At the same time, some parents of teens admit they also struggle with the allure of screens: 36% say they themselves spend too much time on their cellphone. And 51% of teens say they often or sometimes find their parent or caregiver to be distracted by their own cellphone when they are trying to have a conversation with them."

So, the bottom line is in setting parameters for your children, you also need to set limits for yourself. Make sure to emphasize in-person communication, socialization, creativity, and the outdoors over screen time.

PARENT ACTION PLAN: Remind your child how their constant use of digital devices affects those around them. It doesn't allow them to be emotionally available to others, comes across as if they don't care, and can be construed as disrespectful. These attributes will not translate well in adulthood.

CHILD'S LESSON LEARNED: I understand that I need to limit my use of devices, and in social situations, I am aware of how using them translates to others. I need to be aware that eye contact is an important aspect of in-person communication.

SOCIAL MEDIA OVERVIEW

Whether you like it or not, you need to know all about social media. How can you monitor what you don't know?

The problem is that it changes frequently, but it's important to keep up with the trends. I was told several years ago, unbeknownst to me, that Facebook is for "old people." I was shocked when my students told me that. I went home, and my own children confirmed it. "Mom, kids don't use Facebook. That's for parents."

I remember when MySpace was the precursor to Facebook, and then Vine lasted for a hot minute. Social media changes so quickly that it can seem overwhelming to try and keep up with the latest trends.

The major social media apps that are being used at the time of this writing are YouTube, TikTok, Instagram, Twitter, Snapchat, and Facebook.

The average time people spend on social media is three hours per day. There are close to four billion active users of social media all over the world. Did you know that all of these apps require children to be at least 13 years old or have parental consent to use them?

If your child is under 13 and has a social media app that you aren't aware of, they may have used a false birthdate to get an account.

YouTube

YouTube was developed in 2005 and has 2 billion users worldwide. If your child has an account and is between the ages of 13-17, they must have parental consent. The videos that pop up there are hit and miss. Your child could be innocently looking for a video on something benign and see an inappropriate video show up as a suggested video. If your child needs to use YouTube for an assignment, make sure you are monitoring what they're doing.

If your child has a YouTube account, it should be private with comments turned off.

A safer alternative is YouTube Kids, which anyone can use, and adult content is filtered. Unfortunately, there have been stories of inappropriate content making its way on this platform as well.

Again, kids should be accessing these sites in an open area where you can monitor their activity.

Keep in mind that what looks innocent on YouTube may be more subversive. "BBC Trending has found hundreds of similar videos of children's cartoon characters with inappropriate themes. In addition to Peppa Pig, there are similar videos featuring characters from the Disney movie Frozen, the Minions franchise, Doc McStuffins, Thomas the Tank Engine, and many more."

This is especially disturbing if you're thinking your young child is innocently looking up cartoon videos. Make sure your child is on restricted mode, and if you see that an inappropriate video makes it through the filter, flag it immediately. YouTube will take it down, but it usually takes a few hours.

TikTok

Launched in 2016 in China, TikTok took the American market by storm in 2018 when it merged with Musical.ly. TikTok now has over 800 million users globally, with the app being downloaded 1.5 billion times. It allows users to upload 15-second videos with music clips.

This app has had security flaws, allowing hackers to see personal information and manipulate content. Some U.S. military branches have banned TikTok because of security issues. There is also inappropriate content that anyone can view.

If your teen is going to use it, it should be on restricted mode to limit inappropriate content, the account should be switched from public to private, and you should be following them.

At the time of this writing, President Donald Trump considered banning the app from the United States, and Microsoft was deliberating purchasing the app.

Common Sense Media warns, "When you sign up for TikTok, your account is public by default, meaning anyone can see your videos, send you direct messages, and use your location information."

For this reason, parents must change these settings immediately.

Instagram

Instagram is a platform, featuring short videos and photos, that was created in 2010 by Kevin Systrom and Michael Krieger. It is one of the more popular sites with 130 million users globally. Owned by Facebook, this app can be linked to your Facebook page.

Make sure your teen's profile is on private, and again, be careful of fake accounts trying to follow them. There are many bots and spam accounts that try to procure private information.

Be aware of the accounts they are following. There are many accounts that seem harmless, but when you scroll through them, it's anything but innocent; there are accounts with pornography, ones that encourage inappropriate behavior (e.g., eating disorders), and so forth.

Discuss with your teen that Instagram may not be good for their mental health. "A survey of almost 1,500 14 to 24-year-olds found that the photo-sharing platform has a serious impact on young people's body image and the quality and quantity of sleep they get. It also contributes to bullying, anxiety, depression, and a genuine fear of missing out that makes it difficult to disconnect, the research by the Royal Society for Public Health (RSPH) and the Young Health Movement (YHM) found."

Because many photos on this site are filtered, photoshopped, and made to look "perfect," this can give a false sense of reality.

At the time of publication, Instagram just launched its version of TikTok called Instagram Reels, with 15-second videos and sound clips.

Twitter

Twitter is a microblogging platform that was launched in 2006 by former Google employees Evan Williams, Jack Dorsey, and Noah Glass. It began with a limitation of 140 characters per Tweet but has since been doubled to 280. There are currently 81 million users, with 336 million monthly active users.

The demographic of users tends to be 18-plus, but just like with every social media app, they have to be really careful what they post here. You can also have a private

PARENTING TEENS IN A DIGITAL WORLD

profile, so tweets are not made public. Because of the ease with which users can post and reply, there are many instances of not thinking beforehand and making inappropriate posts that can cause issues in the future. Famous comedian and actor Kevin Hart was removed from hosting the 2019 Oscars for homophobic tweets he posted in 2011.

Tech Advisor points out some of the downsides of Twitter for teens: "However, the main factor which makes Twitter unsuitable for kids is that there's no content filtering—the company doesn't screen for or remove offensive tweets—so kids could, and likely will, see inappropriate language and images. If a brand has a Twitter account, they can prevent underage people from following them, but again it's simple to enter a fake birthdate to get around this."

In my opinion, I don't think Twitter is an appropriate social media outlet for young teens.

Snapchat

Business of Apps states, "Snapchat is an image and video messaging app developed by Stanford University students Evan Spiegel, Bobby Murphy, and Reggie Brown in 2011. It allows users to capture and send 'Snaps' that are only viewable for a set duration of 1 to 10 seconds or until closed by the recipient, after which they are automatically deleted. Originally, this was just photos; video capability was added in 2012."

There are 46 million Snapchat users, and with this app, the photo that is sent disappears once it's opened. However, people can take screenshots of what was sent. It's important to only allow friends to see content from Snapchat.

Common Sense Media states, "The biggest challenge for parents is that there's no way to see your kid's activity in the app in the same way as on other social media platforms. Since there's no feed to scroll, there's not much to monitor. Instead, focus on privacy settings."

Facebook

Begun in 2004 by Harvard student Mark Zuckerberg, Facebook is one of the oldest social media sites. Even though Facebook seems to be for an older demographic, it is still a top contender with close to 170 million users globally.

If your teen has an account, it is important to go into the privacy settings and limit all content to either "only me" or "friends only." You can even do a preview of what the page would look like to a stranger.

Make sure your teen is aware of fake accounts trying to friend them—even duplicates of people they know. Make sure their friends' list is hidden for this reason and tell them to only accept friendships with people they have verified.

Their profile should be private, and you should be their first friend.

According to CNET, "The five hidden dangers of Facebook are:

Your information is being shared with third parties

Privacy settings revert to a less safe default mode after each redesign

Facebook ads may contain malware (virus)

Your real friends unknowingly make you vulnerable (to hackers/viruses)

Scammers are creating fake profiles."

Other apps

Other apps parents should know: Tumblr, Tinder, Whatsapp, Facebook Messenger, Google Hangouts, Reddit, and Kik, among many, many others. If you do a quick search of Kik, for example, it will bring up all kinds of anonymous chat apps that are alarming.

Remember, your children are watching you. If they see that you don't care about their digital use or are ill-informed about it, they may try to take advantage of that fact. Parents need to be proactive, informed, and engaged with their teens. But we must be careful not to be overbearing and disrespectful. We ultimately get what we give.

If you suspect something is terribly wrong, then it is up to you to take the bull by the horns and investigate. The tools are there—you just need to know about them.

PARENT ACTION PLAN: Do your own research on these apps. Give parameters on what you want to allow your teen to use. Make sure you have an account and are following them and have login information.

CHILD'S LESSON LEARNED: My parents are no dummies and are on top of what is out there. They must really care about me and what I'm doing.

THE CHALLENGES OF SOCIAL MEDIA

I once heard someone say that allowing your child access to social media is like dropping them off in Times Square at 2 a.m. and driving off.

That visual really stuck with me and disturbed me. Because it's true. Times Square may offer an abundance of innocent entertainment, but there is also a darker and seedier side to it.

Social media is a very tricky medium. It's a great way to connect with friends and family who live afar, but there's a dangerous side too.

There are too many terrible stories of online child predators, and I don't need to delve into that here. Just read the news, and you'll see these stories on the daily of adults taking advantage of children online.

But one thing we don't talk about too much is body image and self-esteem, for both girls and boys.

A quick scroll through Instagram shows you all of the beautifully crafted, photoshopped pictures of men and women looking almost too good to be true.

When your teen looks at these images, do you think it makes them feel good about themselves or insecure and unattractive?

When they try to emulate the Kylie Jenners and Chris Hemsworths of the world, it's just not realistic, and it makes them feel inadequate. Instead of embracing their differences, they only see what they feel are shortcomings.

It not only gives them idealistic expectations for themselves, but it also gives them impractical expectations of others, which can lead to a road of disappointment and feelings of inadequacy.

Make sure they understand what went on behind the scenes before someone posted these photos—filters, Photoshop, lighting, and so forth.

I'm not saying don't allow them to be on social media, but make sure they are over 13, you are their first follower, you have access to their login information, and you limit their time on it. Again, if they're using it, they should be in front of you—not behind closed doors.

By ensuring they're not using it behind closed doors and overnight, you can help prevent an addiction to it.

The BBC ties body image issues and social media together: "Using social media does appear to be correlated with body image concerns. A systematic review of 20 papers published in 2016 found that photo-based activities, like scrolling through Instagram or posting pictures of yourself, were a particular problem when it came to negative thoughts about your body."

This can lead to depression, anxiety, insecurity, and eating disorders in both girls and boys. Remember, girls are not the only ones vulnerable to these things.

Another frightening aspect of social media is groups that encourage children to harm themselves (or others), commit suicide, or develop eating disorders.

We've seen children take part in things like the Tide Pod challenge, where children ate laundry detergent pods, risking their health, as some sort of a dare. Remember what I discussed earlier regarding the lack of development of the prefrontal cortex in adolescence? Teens lack the ability to see the consequences of their actions and are more prone to act impulsively.

On social media, there are also groups that promote anorexia, bulimia, and cutting. With teens being so vulnerable to peer pressure, this is concerning.

"The most popular social media sites have since 2012 outlined policies for images or posts about self-harm, whether glorifying cutting, suicide or eating disorders like anorexia and bulimia. But a search of related terms still can yield pictures of cut wrists and more graphic images that could be triggering for people inclined to harm themselves."

I want to reiterate that I am not anti-technology. However, I feel that in order for parents to fully understand how important it is to be an active part of their children's online activity, they need to be made aware of all of the dangerous possibilities.

On the plus side, social media gives teens an outlet to socialize with peers, feel less isolated, and learn about cultural and political affairs. This is a reason why children need to learn digital citizenship—to allow them to navigate the Internet as an educated and critically thinking audience.

PARENT ACTION PLAN: If your teen already has social media accounts, make sure you have their login information and that you are following them. Encourage them to follow uplifting and body-positive accounts.

CHILD'S LESSON LEARNED: My parents are looking out for me, and they make sure to be a part of my life.

CYBERBULLYING

Teens feel that being on social media can help forge close relationships with people, but it can also bring a lot of unnecessary drama in their lives.

Since their maturity levels are not fully developed, they may be unable to manage interactions, jealousies, and judgments. They can be reactive, cruel, and irrational when it comes to behaving on social media, and this can cause problems on many different levels—personal, social, school, and others.

As many times as we tell them that what you post on the Internet is never deleted (even if you delete it), they may have issues with impulsivity, which can lead to troubles down the road.

How many times have we seen celebrities under fire for something they tweeted 10 years ago? It never goes away.

I know I can speak for teachers and guidance counselors around the country that a lot of the drama we see in school stems from the Internet. I have taken part in roundtable interventions between students and parents trying to get to the bottom of who said what. Students can be very cruel when they post online, not thinking of the ramifications their words have on the person they're attacking.

The scary part about cyberbullying is that it can be done from an anonymous account, so you don't know who is doing it. Someone could even hack into your account and post terrible things to make it look like you did it.

Just recently, a 17-year-old Florida teenager was arrested for hacking many Twitter accounts, including the accounts of Barack Obama, Joe Biden, Elon Musk, Bill Gates, and Kanye West. This teen was able to access the accounts of these very high-profile people and write tweets from their accounts.

This just highlights the security issues that are exposed with these various apps.

Another term we hear a lot is "keyboard warrior," which is defined as a person who makes abusive or aggressive posts on the Internet, typically concealing their true identity.

Because the person is anonymous, they feel they have the power to be even more callous with their words.

This type of behavior could result in criminal consequences and can adversely affect your child's standing with schools and their future.

Cyberbullying is widespread: "Over half of adolescents and teens have been bullied online, and about the same number have engaged in cyberbullying. More than 1 in 3 young people have experienced cyberthreats online. Over 25 percent of adolescents and teens have been bullied repeatedly through their cell phones or the Internet. Well over half of young people do not tell their parents when cyberbullying occurs."

Those are some frightening statistics, especially since most teens do not share with their parents if this is occurring. Remember, besides the news feed that you see, they could be receiving DMs (direct messages) that are hidden from view. This is where a lot of bullying can take place, so you may never see it. This is another reason why it is important you keep talking to your teen and make it a safe space for them to share anything that is going on. I know this doesn't guarantee that you'll find out about it, but your child will feel more empowered to do the right thing if you've spoken about hypothetical situations pertaining to this before giving them their devices.

PARENT ACTION PLAN: Explain what cyberbullying is and have an open dialogue about the importance of reporting it and taking screenshots of it. Also, explain the consequences of engaging in cyberbullying behavior.

CHILD'S LESSON LEARNED: I know that I can trust my parents if I should be a victim of cyberbullying. I also know that this is unacceptable behavior that can have major consequences outside the home.

RESTRICTIONS

When you purchase a smartphone, or any device for that matter, you should find out all of the parental controls that you can initiate on the device.

Those Genius Bar employees at Apple are there for a reason. They will go over the settings and controls for you so that you know what options are available. Anywhere you buy your phone should have employees that can assist you with restrictions.

You can also use outside companies, such as Web Watcher and Norton, and apps that can be used on both Android and iOS devices like FamilyTime, Qustodio, and Our Pact.

According to Digital Trends, "FamilyTime does everything, allowing you to customize precisely what content your kids should have access to, set time limits, track location, and more. The software gives you tools to set homework and bedtimes, or just limit the total time your kids spend on their phones. There's also support for geofencing so you get alerts when a phone enters or leaves a specific area, and location tracking, so you can see exactly where your child is. On top of that, you can block or control usage on an app-by-app basis, apply internet filters, monitor calls and texts, and keep an eye on contact lists."

Knowledge is power. There are many tools out there to assist parents in controlling what their children see, but it is up to us to do the work to find and implement them. Of course, every relationship between parent and child is unique, and you may trust one child more than another, but be aware of your options.

Another way you can restrict usage is to put your family Wi-Fi on a timer so that it can only be accessed during specific times during the day.

I provide you with various links to digital parenting resources in the back of this book.

PARENT ACTION PLAN: Research and select a monitoring app and/or website on all your child's devices. Make your child aware of this. Communication is key—if you do it secretly in order to have a "gotcha" moment, the line of trust with your child will be damaged.

CHILD'S LESSON LEARNED: I am not tempted to do anything wrong on my devices since my parents are monitoring everything I'm doing.

HOW TEENS HIDE WHAT THEY'RE DOING

I learned very quickly how teens can hide what they're doing. Remember, they are savvy and a lot of them know the technology better than you do.

According to CNN Business, 70 percent of teens hide their online activity from their parents. Not only do they hide inappropriate activity (violence, porn, etc.), but they also know how to hack emails, be in social chats with strangers, and use their phones to cheat in school.

The CNN article highlights the top ways teens hide their online activity:

1. Clear browser history (53 percent)

2. Close/minimize browser when parent walked in (46 percent)
3. Hide or delete IMs [instant messages] or videos (34 percent)
4. Lie or omit details about online activities (23 percent)
5. Use a computer their parents don't check (23 percent)
6. Use an Internet-enabled mobile device (21 percent)
7. Use privacy settings to make certain content viewable only by friends (20 percent)
8. Use private browsing modes (20 percent)

I remember many years ago when a student hacked into the principal's emails and was also able to go into the digital gradebook and change his grades. This was a young teenage student who had enough tech knowledge to do this.

I have heard of middle school students accessing all kinds of porn on their school devices, thinking the school technology officer wouldn't find it. They also secretly download games, take photos of themselves and others (without them knowing), and join online groups that encourage eating disorders or self-harm.

This is why it's important for you to know what they are doing. I hear some parents claim they do not want to invade their child's privacy. I have never understood this argument. Since when is a minor's privacy more important than their safety?

I believe the right to privacy is earned, and your child's age, maturity level, and school efforts should play a role in that. If parents suspect foul play on their child's part, it is the right of the parent to intervene.

Even when children are right in front of you, they can hide their behavior. They can conceal their toolbar and switch tabs lightning quick. Some students lower the screen's brightness so much that you can't see their screen unless you are directly behind them. Don't allow them to do this. Tell them to turn their brightness up. Trust me on this one.

As a teacher, I love the tool Apple Classroom. With this tool, I am able to see all of my student's iPad screens as they work, and I have the ability to lock their device if I see any sign of trouble. It's quite powerful and truly limits the amount of distracting behavior students engage in.

Another way your child can hide what they're doing is by using ghost apps. These are apps that appear to be one thing, such as a calculator or settings app, but when accessed via password are apps that can hide photos and videos from adults. In addition, there are ghost apps that can bypass a GPS tracker and make it look like your child is in a different location than where they actually are. So, if you are using a GPS tracker on your child, you need to make sure they are not using a ghost app to trick you.

Again, these are merely options and suggestions depending on your relationship with your child. I believe there is a sliding scale of trust you have based on your child's age and maturity level, and some of these options may seem a bit extreme.

The point is to make sure you are keeping up with ever-changing technology in case there does come a time when you need to intervene. Kids seem to be several steps ahead of adults when it comes to digital expertise.

PARENT ACTION PLAN: Educate yourself on the various ways your child can hide their activity. Talk to them about it and the potential repercussions if you should find out that they are concealing what they're doing. Make sure to keep communication lines open and to not overreact when dealing with your teen.

CHILD'S LESSON LEARNED: My parents are well informed when it comes to how people hide their online activity. Since they are open with me and respect my privacy, I am encouraged to do the right thing when it comes to online activity. If I do stumble upon something, I know I can talk to them openly without judgment.

THE ZOOM WORLD

On Friday, March 13, 2020, school administrators told me to pack up my things and be prepared to teach remotely temporarily until we could "flatten the curve" during the Covid-19 pandemic outbreak. Little did I know it wouldn't be a 2-week temporary hiatus from the classroom. I ended up teaching via Zoom for almost 3 months.

At the current moment of writing this book (August 2020), I don't know if I'm going back to teaching in the classroom, using a blended combination of classroom and Zoom, or doing Zoom classes only in the fall.

What I do know is that remote learning may become a more common form of teaching in my future, so I thought I would include some words of advice as far as virtual classroom etiquette are concerned.

Please, do not allow your children to Zoom in their bedrooms. They should be in an open area just like any other time where you or another adult can monitor their behavior. It is too tempting for children to be distracted by other things like chatting, games, and items in their bedroom if there is no one watching them.

Have them treat remote learning like they are in a classroom—no eating, sitting like they're lounging, or getting up whenever they want.

I noticed that even some of my best students were distracted with no adult supervision. Students don't realize how obvious it is to the teacher when they are on their phones texting, chatting through iMessage, or playing video games during a Zoom call. All I have to do is randomly call on a student, and I know right away if they're paying attention to the lesson or not.

Teachers, I beseech you to think about what your students are feeling during remote learning. Watching my 13-year-old son sit in a chair all day with little ability to get up and move around was disheartening. Remember, at a regular brick-and-mortar school, students have the opportunity to move, walk, and socialize. Zoom fatigue and burnout are real.

Four tips for teachers:

Begin class with a quick mindful minute to establish focus. A mindful minute is a moment to focus on breath and do nothing but relax the body and quiet the mind.

After 20 minutes, provide a stretch break. Allow them to get up, walk around, stretch, and move their bodies.

Don't keep students until the end of class.

Instead, allow students to get off the call and work independently.

I don't believe remote learning should have the same hours as a regular school day—are you listening, school districts? Eight-hour school days should *not* apply to remote learning—that is torturous for not only the students but also the teachers.

If the class is designed for 60 minutes, students shouldn't be expected to sit on the call from beginning to end. I taught for 20 to 25 minutes, provided a break, opened up for questions for 5 to 10 minutes, and then I would stay on the call if students needed individual assistance. If not, they were excused to go and work on their classwork/homework.

It's just not fair to keep a child sitting at a computer the entire amount of time. Remember, they have multiple 60-minute classes per day in remote learning.

Some administrators forget that there are many teachers who not only have to teach from home but then must help their own children with their remote learning. The line between teacher/parent and work/home becomes quite conflated.

I honestly don't know how my colleagues with really little ones are doing it. I'm grateful that my older children are grown and done with school and that my youngest is 13 and quite self-sufficient.

PARENT ACTION PLAN: Homeschooling parents and teachers, be cognizant of the amount of time you are keeping children seated in front of the screen.

CHILD'S LESSON LEARNED: My parents and teachers care about my well-being, and I can focus better knowing they will not expect me to sit for an entire 60-minute session on the computer multiple times a day.

MY INTERVIEW WITH DR. ELIZABETH MILOVIDOV

While researching and writing this book, I was fortunate to connect with a leader in child online protection and, more specifically, digital parenting. Her name is Dr. Elizabeth Milovidov, and she is an attorney, law professor, and e-safety consultant based in Paris, France. Her website digitalparentingcoach.com serves a broad audience and gives insight into Internet safety for parents by providing them with bite-sized information dealing with a wide scope of issues. Based on her lengthy experience in the Internet safety domain, she has created guides, toolkits, and other digital downloads for parents and caregivers. She credits her understanding of parental issues in the online protection area to consulting projects for technology companies, governments, and schools.

Dr. Milovidov was gracious enough to allow me to interview her and add her voice to my conversation on this topic. Overall, she sees the same problems in Europe that we have in the United States with regard to responsible online use. She was adamant about the term "responsible online use" because she feels that "online safety" has become synonymous with restricted or no technology use. One of her current projects is for the Council of Europe, where the expert working group is trying to create a digital citizenship curriculum for the forty-seven member countries.

The concept of digital citizenship is crucial yet often misunderstood. Many believe that digital citizenship *is* online safety, but it is actually a blend of media and information literacy, security, privacy, critical thinking skills, and more. Parents may think that schools are teaching digital citizenship, but that is not always necessarily the case. Many educators are dealing with a full teaching load and may not be able (or technically capable) of introducing digital citizenship and other concepts for the digital age.

Dr. Milovidov believes that basic concepts of digital citizenship can be and should be taught at home starting at a very early age. She says that many parents seek advice when it's too late and a problem arises, instead of being proactive before anything can go wrong. Parents should teach their children online strategies just like they would teach them any other life strategy—like going to the store or playing in the park. In the digital space, there is a great need for a blend of positive parenting and prevention and awareness parenting, if such a term could exist.

As a mother to two tech-savvy children, she notes that her children's devices are ultimately hers, although she respects her children's "right to play, right to participate, right to learn" in the digital age. However, access to those devices can be restricted or indeed removed altogether as a repercussion for poor choices. One of the ways that Dr. Milovidov ensures that her children can make "responsible" choices is by keeping the lines of communication open and transparent. In her opinion, the key to success when dealing with digital use is the importance of communication with your child.

Dr. Milovidov says the goal is for your child to be open with you if they do stumble upon something inappropriate or have been cyberbullied. Just as your children can share the positive and beneficial experiences that occur online, they should be supported to share the negative instances as well. It's when your child is secretive when the problems really occur. If parents are having those conversations and supporting their children through the good and bad, parents are in a much better position to help their children safely navigate the digital space.

It's vital to understand that children should not have access to digital devices overnight. One of the things that digital experts, including Dr. Milovidov, are seeing are children gaming at all hours of the night because of friends in different time zones. In addition to having overnight access, there is something enticing with a digital device in a darkened room, late at night. Parents can remember their own experiences chatting on the phone late at night to help them understand the attractiveness of this kind of intimacy. Being aware of these types of challenges can help parents create a supportive environment for their digital families.

Once we've taken care of children getting a good night's sleep, we can then consider some of the problems that doctors are seeing such as eyesight and neck strain, obesity, and not getting enough fresh air.

I questioned Dr. Milovidov about what she sees as the three most essential safety tips for parents:

1. Open a transparent line of communication with your children. When children are not talking and parents are not asking, it is difficult, if not impossible, to handle issues and challenges of the online world. Refer to part 1 of this book and remember some of the key components of keeping a solid connection with your child.

2. Parents need to stay informed about what's happening in technology—privacy settings, new app updates, and so forth. There are plenty of web-

sites that offer newsletters to help keep you up to date on the latest technology information. I will be giving you some specific websites at the end of this book that I highly recommend and encourage you to explore.

3. Be respectful of your child's data protection and privacy from strangers. Parents need to understand their child's privacy settings and think about their child's digital safety, whenever their children have a presence online—whether their photos are being taken, whether they are playing online, and so forth. Be aware of what your child is doing online. Remind your child that whatever they do remains on the Internet. Dr. Milovidov says she reminds older teens to do a social media cleanse by going back and deleting anything that could hinder their chances of getting into a school or gaining a job. Sometimes what they post at the age of 14 is not something they would want to be seen at 18—not necessarily inappropriate but possibly immature.

When asked about the prevalent problems that appear online, Dr. Milovidov says she sees a misperception between what parents see as being the real dangers on the Internet versus what children see as the problem. Parents see the immediate problem as "stranger danger"—that their child will be kidnapped by someone they've met online never to be seen again. Obviously, that is a real threat and should be taken seriously. Nevertheless, their children will most likely say that they're more concerned with cyberbullying, hoaxes (such as Momo or Jonny Galindo), and challenges (like the Blue Whale challenge).

If you don't know what these hoaxes or challenges are, make sure to do some online research.

In addition, children are worried about seeing something like porn and not knowing what to do, or they're afraid of being asked to do something they are not comfortable with while trying to seem like the "cool kid."

Undoubtedly, these issues that worry children can be dealt with if parents keep an open channel of communication. Children should feel safe and comfortable talking to you about these concerns, and you should be knowledgeable enough on these topics to explain to your child what they should do if they experience any of these difficulties.

As a consultant, Dr. Milovidov works with e-Enfance, the French child online protection association that runs Net Ecoute, the French Helpline. As part of her work, she meets with other members of the INSAFE network (a project sponsored by the European commission that brings together twenty-seven member countries). Twice a year, the INSAFE network meets to go over the data and share best practices in online safety. INSAFE has consistently noticed the majority of the calls that come in (from children) deal with cyberbullying.

She notes that if you spoke with someone from law enforcement, they may have an entirely different answer. Currently, with the pandemic and more children home online, there is a surge in online predatory behavior.

This alarming statistic should serve as additional motivation for you to be aware of what your child is doing online. Predators go where children are, and left on their own, your child will be vulnerable.

A few years ago, Dr. Milovidov attended a digital parenting facilitator workshop with The Parent Zone, experts in digital family life, and said they have a formula called the 3 Ws, which assists parents in answering simple questions about their child in the digital world.

1.   *What* are they doing online?
2.   *Who* are they going online to speak with?
3.   *Where* are they going online?

  *Dr. Milovidov added a fourth: *When* are they going online (late at night, with the babysitter, etc.)?

These four questions alone can give parents an enormous amount of information about their child's online usage. If you can begin with these four basics, the rest should fall into place.

In discussing compassion and kindness in the Internet space, although there is not a lot of evidence-based research on how social media is affecting these character traits, we have seen that social-emotional learning needs to happen at an early age. Dr. Milovidov was involved in the 2-year ENABLE project designed to tackle bullying by emphasizing social and emotional learning. During their research of children 11 to 14-years-old in six European countries, they learned that teaching social and emotional learning at 11-years-old may be too late. A better model might be to look at Denmark, where they begin teaching children as young as three years old about kindness and empathy.

It's also vital for parents to model that for their children—not ignoring people by being on their device and not yelling at people on the phone, in a Zoom call, or even when even talking to Alexa. Why model poor behavior toward a robot?

Online disinhibition is a factor with people (children and adults) who feel empowered by being behind a keyboard. They say things that they wouldn't say in a face-to-face confrontation (aka keyboard warrior as mentioned in chapter 19).

At the same time, Dr. Milovidov mentions that technology provides a way for those children who are shy or have social anxiety to build relationships online. She and I both love technology and all of the ways it can benefit our children, but it's essential to remain informed and aware of the potential challenges.

FINAL THOUGHTS

I know parents feel they have enough to worry about, but not learning about technology and the ins and outs of ensuring your child's safety is akin to digging your head in the sand.

First and foremost, you need to build trust and an open line of communication with your child. Without that, trying to set guidelines and boundaries will fall on deaf ears. Your child needs to know they can come to you at any time and be honest with anything that happened. They also need to feel as if you are creating rules for their own safety. Do not come across like a dictator; instead, act like a parent who loves and watches out for their child.

Second, make sure you are educated on the technology that you are giving your child. Don't just hand them a device and allow them to fend for themselves. Like I've said before, this is a recipe for disaster and will only create a more strained relationship with your child as they will become more secretive and use screen time to avoid real communication.

Finally, be diligent about monitoring your child's Internet activity.

Technology is a wonderful tool to learn, engage, and connect with others. Being informed about it shouldn't be a daunting task. There are plenty of resources out there that provide bite-sized information regarding anything and everything having to do with technology.

Check out these great websites for parents:

- **commonsensemedia.org**—an excellent resource for parents and educators on everything you need to know about digital citizenship
- **commonsense.org/education/digital-glossary**—an extensive list of definitions for various acronyms and terms used by teens (sometimes to hide things)
- **digitalparentingcoach.com**—Elizabeth Milovidov's website to help parents navigate the digital world

Other helpful websites:

- internetsafety101.org
- simplecyberlife.com
- culturereframed.org
- connectsafely.org
- parentzone.org.uk

Bibliography

"10 Facts About School Attendance." Attendance Works, 2018. https://www.attendanceworks.org/chronic-absence/the-problem/10-facts-about-school-attendance/.

Arsenault, Leanne. "Podcast: Research on Household Chores." APA Divisions, 2017. https://www.apadivisions.org/division-35/news-events/news/household-chores.

CBS Interactive Staff. "Five Hidden Dangers of Facebook (Q&A)." CNET, May 8, 2010. https://www.cnet.com/news/five-hidden-dangers-of-facebook-q-a/.

Clement, J. "Most Popular Social Media Apps in U.S." Statista, July 16, 2020. https://www.statista.com/statistics/248074/most-popular-us-social-networking-apps-ranked-by-audience/.

Conger, Kate, and Nathaniel Popper. "Florida Teenager Is Charged as 'Mastermind' of Twitter Hack." *New York Times*, July 31, 2020. https://www.nytimes.com/2020/07/31/technology/twitter-hack-arrest.html.

"Cyber Bullying Statistics." Bullying Statistics, July 7, 2015. http://www.bullyingstatistics.org/content/cyber-bullying-statistics.html.

Dallas, Mary Elizabeth. "Ban Electronics in Kids' Bedrooms, Expert Says." Consumer HealthDay, September 26, 2014. https://consumer.healthday.com/health-technology-information-18/computers-in-

ternet-144/ban-electronics-in-kids-bedrooms-ex-
pert-says-691503.html.

"Data & Statistics." Centers for Disease Control and
Prevention, March 13, 2019. https://www.cdc.gov/
features/datastatistics.html?CDC_AA_ref-
Val=https%3A%2F%2Fwww.cdc.gov%2Ffea-
tures%2Fdsdrowsydriving%2Findex.html.

"Education Data Release: One in Every Five Children,
Adolescents and Youth Is Out of School." UNESCO
Institute of Statistics, March 22, 2018.
http://uis.unesco.org/en/news/education-data-re-
lease-one-every-five-children-adolescents-and-
youth-out-school.

Elgersma, Christine. "Parents' Ultimate Guide to
Snapchat." Common Sense Media, March 1, 2020.
https://www.commonsensemedia.org/blog/par-
ents-ultimate-guide-to-snapchat.

"Family Media Agreement: Common Sense Media."
Common Sense Media, 2018. https://www.com-
monsensemedia.org/family-media-agreement.

Forrest, Sharita. "Study: Families Spend Half of Their
Evening Meal Distracted by Technology, Tasks."
Medical Xpress, April 2, 2019. https://medicalx-
press.com/news/2019-04-families-evening-meal-
distracted-technology.html.

"Giving Thanks Can Make You Happier." Harvard
Health, 2020. https://www.health.harvard.edu/
healthbeat/giving-thanks-can-make-you-happier.

Grant, Adam, and Allison Sweet Grant. "Stop Trying to
Raise Successful Kids." Atlantic, November 4, 2019.
https://www.theatlantic.com/magazine/archive/
2019/12/stop-trying-to-raise-successful-kids/
600751/.

Gray, Jasmin. "Instagram Ranked 'Most Dangerous' Social Media App For Young People's Mental Health." HuffPost, May 19, 2017.

Hess, Abigail J. "50% Of Teachers Surveyed Say They've Considered Quitting, Blaming Pay, Stress and Lack of Respect." CNBC, August 9, 2019. https://www.cnbc.com/2019/08/09/50percent-of-teachers-surveyed-say-theyve-considered-quitting-teaching.html.

Hill, Simon. "The Best Parental Control Apps for Android and IOS." Digital Trends, May 23, 2020. https://www.digitaltrends.com/mobile/best-parental-control-apps/.

"Internet Addiction: Too Much Time on the Internet for Kids." The Center for Parenting Education, 2020. https://centerforparentingeducation.org/library-of-articles/kids-and-technology/how-much-time-internet-kids/.

Iqbal, Mansoor. "Snap Inc. Revenue and Usage Statistics (2020)." Business of Apps, July 30, 2020. https://www.businessofapps.com/data/snapchat-statistics/.

Jiang, Jingjing. "How Teens and Parents Navigate Screen Time and Device Distractions." Pew Research Center, May 30, 2020. https://www.pewresearch.org/internet/2018/08/22/how-teens-and-parents-navigate-screen-time-and-device-distractions/.

Kamenetz, Anya. "It's A Smartphone Life: More Than Half of U.S. Children Now Have One." NPR, October 31, 2019. https://www.npr.org/2019/10/31/774838891/its-a-smartphone-life-more-than-half-of-u-s-children-now-have-one.

Leonard, Kimberly. "Is Social Media Making Self-Harm Worse for Teens?" U.S. News & World Report,

May 29, 2015. https://www.usnews.com/news/articles/2015/05/29/is-social-media-making-self-harm-worse-for-teens.

Martin, Jim. "Here's What You Need to Know about Twitter and If It's Safe for Kids to Use." Tech Advisor, March 20, 2018. https://www.techadvisor.co.uk/feature/social-networks/is-twitter-safe-for-kids-3671084/.

Mayo Clinic Staff. "Teen Sleep: Why Is Your Teen So Tired?" Mayo Clinic, August 25, 2017. https://www.mayoclinic.org/healthy-lifestyle/tween-and-teen-health/in-depth/teens-health/art-20046157.

"Movies That Inspire Integrity." Common Sense Media. https://www.commonsensemedia.org/lists/movies-that-inspire-integrity.

Oakes, Kelly. "The Complicated Truth about Social Media and Body Image." BBC, March 11, 2019. https://www.bbc.com/future/article/20190311-how-social-media-affects-body-image.

Office of Adolescent Health. "Communicating." US Department of Health and Human Services, March 25, 2019. https://www.hhs.gov/ash/oah/adolescent-development/healthy-relationships/parents-child/communicating/index.html.

"Plagiarism: Facts & Stats." Plagiarism.org RSS, June 7, 2017. https://www.plagiarism.org/article/plagiarism-facts-and-stats.

Rector, Kevin. "Online Child Sex Abuse Reports Surge as Kids Spend More Time on Computers amid Coronavirus." *Los Angeles Times*, May 21, 2020. https://www.latimes.com/california/story/2020-05-21/child-sex-abuse-and-exploitation-surge-online-amid-pandemic-overwhelming-police.

Romero, Carissa. *What We Know About Growth Mindset from Scientific Research*. Stanford, California: Mindset Scholars Network, 2015.

Scharf, June. "What Teens Are Hiding on Their Phones (And What You Can Do About It)." Your Teen Magazine, October 7, 2019. https://yourteenmag.com/technology/ghost-apps-to-hide-online.

Stieg, Cory. "Kids with 'Helicopter Parents' More Likely to Burn Out, Have a Harder Time Transitioning to 'Real World.'" CNBC, November 22, 2019. https://www.cnbc.com/2019/11/22/study-kids-who-have-helicopter-parents-experience-burnout-in-school.html.

Subedar, Anisa, and Will Yates. "The Disturbing YouTube Videos That Are Tricking Children." BBC, March 27, 2017. https://www.bbc.com/news/blogs-trending-39381889.

Sutter, John D. "Survey: 70% of Teens Hide Online Behavior from Parents." CNN, June 25, 2012. https://www.cnn.com/2012/06/25/tech/web/mcafee-teen-online-survey/index.html.

Ucciferri, Frannie. "Parents' Ultimate Guide to TikTok." Common Sense Media, July 23, 2020. https://www.commonsensemedia.org/blog/parents-ultimate-guide-to-tiktok.

"What Research Says About Parent Involvement." Responsive Classroom, 2011. https://www.responsive-classroom.org/what-research-says-about-parent-involvement/.

CPSIA information can be obtained
at www.ICGtesting.com
Printed in the USA
LVHW051945191120
672183LV00015B/2500